Published in the UK in 1994 by
Schofield & Sims Limited, Huddersfield, England.

0 7217 5013 3

Occupations

Schofield & Sims Limited Huddersfield.

The Teacher

The school teacher has chosen one of the best professions: teaching children to read, write and do mathematics and helping them to discover things and understand the world in which they live.

In the first school, each teacher usually teaches all subjects.

In schools for older children, there is usually a specialist teacher in each subject: a History teacher, an English teacher, a Science teacher . . .

In the school playground or on the sports field, the PE teacher organises athletics, cricket or football.

Teachers often take their pupils to visit museums and historical sites, and even take them on trips abroad.

3

The Film-Maker

To make a film requires lots of people who do different things. Shooting the film lasts many weeks and takes place in various locations.

The scriptwriter creates the film's story-line. The director turns the script into pictures and directs the actors to make the film.

The lighting-team organises the lights, the sound-crew records the voices and other sounds, and the camera-crew operates the cameras.

The make-up artists, wardrobe staff and hairdressers help the actors to prepare. It is difficult to be an actor. They have to pretend to be happy, unhappy, angry – or even pretend to be aliens!

When filming has finished, the film editors put the film together. They add the sound effects and music chosen by the director.

On Board an Aeroplane

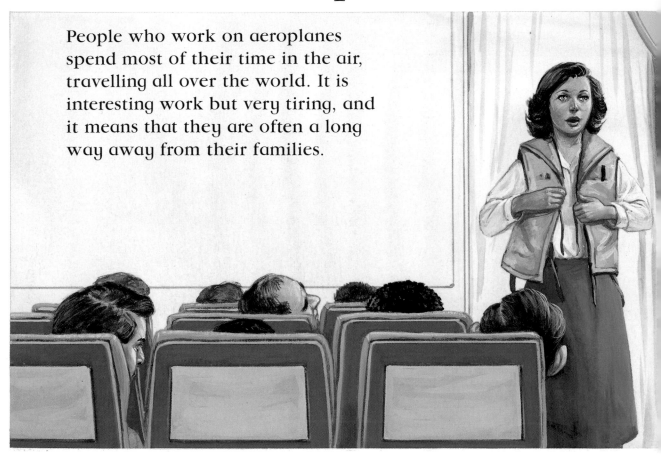

People who work on aeroplanes spend most of their time in the air, travelling all over the world. It is interesting work but very tiring, and it means that they are often a long way away from their families.

The captain flies the aeroplane. He prepares the flight plan, which is the route that he is going to take in the sky to get to the next *airport*.

He is constantly in touch by radio with the air-traffic controllers who are in the *airport* control tower. They guide the aeroplane on take-off and landing.

The copilot studies the weather and makes sure the aircraft has enough fuel. The flight engineer constantly watches the instrument panel.

The cabin crew serves drinks and food to the passengers. They also hand out headphones for the in-flight entertainment.

The Doctor

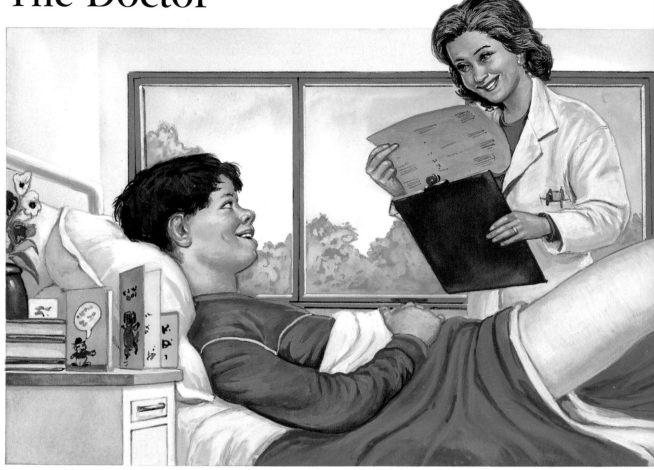

The paediatrician looks after children throughout childhood. On each hospital visit, the child is weighed and measured to make sure he or she is healthy.

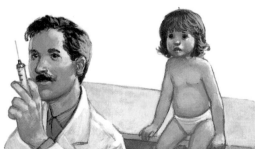

The doctor also vaccinates adults and children. The vaccines protect us against many kinds of illness.

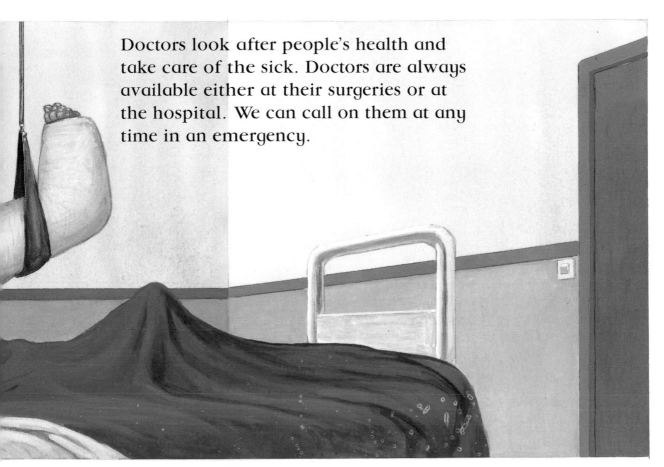

Doctors look after people's health and take care of the sick. Doctors are always available either at their surgeries or at the hospital. We can call on them at any time in an emergency.

When a woman is going to have a baby, she usually goes to hospital. The midwife helps her to give birth.

The surgeon operates on patients. He or she is helped by nurses and a doctor who make sure the sick person does not feel any pain.

The Fire-Fighter

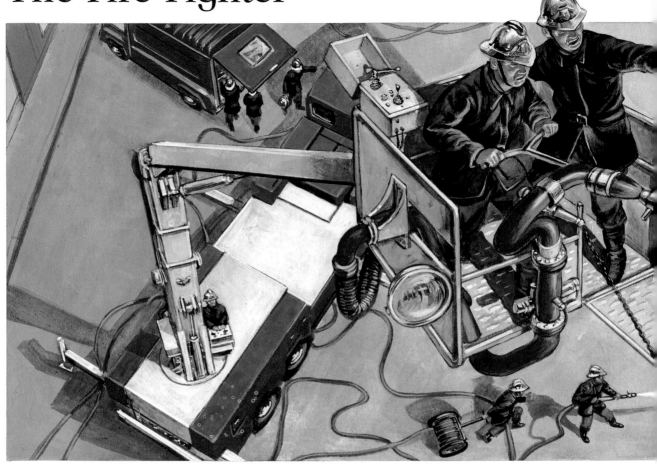

Fire-fighters are well equipped.
They wear special suits and face
masks and use breathing apparatus
when they have to tackle flames.

Fire-fighters also help people
when they are trapped by floods.

Fire-fighters are very brave. Night or day they are ready to help people. When they are called out to a fire, they are usually there within minutes. In each country, the fire-fighter's uniform is different.

Sometimes, fire-fighters are asked to destroy pests such as wasps and hornets.

Some fires happen at sea. Fire-fighters then use specially-equipped ships.

The Vet

Vets are animal doctors. They look after cows, sheep, horses, cats, dogs, birds and other creatures.

In the country, when a cow or a horse is ill, the vet travels to see it. In the car, the vet has surgical instruments and medicines.

Vets can also treat animals in their surgeries. They diagnose illness, take *X-rays* and perform operations.

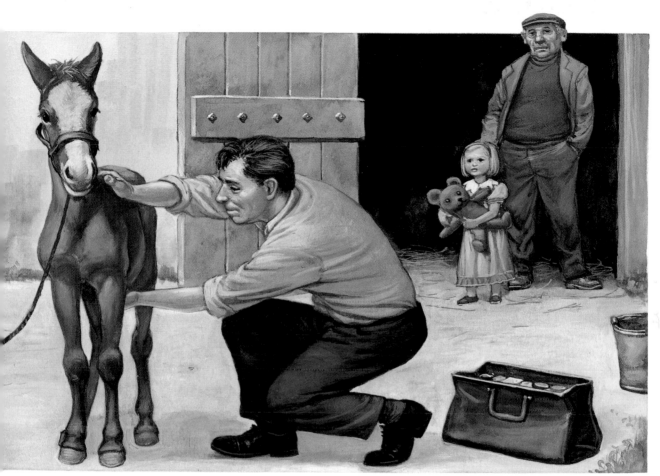

When they operate, vets put on a special coat and plastic gloves. Usually, an assistant helps with the operation.

Sometimes vets work in zoos or wildlife parks. Wild animals have to be *tranquillised* before they can be treated.

The Dancer

Dancing lessons can start at six years old. The first exercises take place at the *barre* to loosen the *muscles* and make them more flexible. The pupil follows the same exercises hundreds of times in front of a mirror to get the movement right, and hold the head and arms properly.

To become a great dancer takes years of hard work. Dancers must be graceful, have a strong physique and have a good sense of rhythm so they can dance in time to the music.

Then the stage exercises start: the jumps, pirouettes, glissades and arabesques. The dancer has to learn to follow the music correctly.

In a ballet, there are usually male dancers. A principal male dancer has to be supple and he must be strong enough to be able to lift and carry a ballerina.

The Astronaut

Astronauts travel in space, and some of them have even been to the moon and back. To travel in space, astronauts must wear a special spacesuit. They carry oxygen to breathe and radios to communicate with each other.

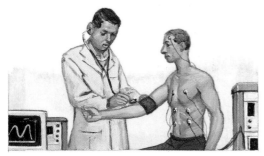

To be an astronaut, you need to be very fit and healthy and have a lot of scientific knowledge.

Taking off in a rocket puts a great strain on the body. To train for this, astronauts use a machine that spins at great speed.

When in space, an astronaut must be able to repair the spacecraft or perform experiments.

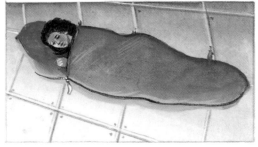

In their space capsule, the astronauts sleep in special bags attached to the cabin wall.

The Journalist

Journalists tell us what is going on in the world. They can work on radio or television or on newspapers and magazines. A sports journalist reports on big sporting events such as football matches.

The photojournalist takes news photographs or films. It can be a dangerous job when they have to go to countries where wars are being fought.

On television, the news presenter gives us the news of the day and shows us pictures taken by the reporters.

Journalists also write articles which appear in newspapers and magazines. They use word processors and computers to prepare their stories for publication.

These days, international news is broadcast to us very quickly because of satellites which transmit words and pictures around the world.

19

The Farmer

In autumn, the farmer turns over the soil using his tractor. Winter wheat can also be sown now. The farm animals have to be taken in at night.

In spring, the farmer ploughs the fields before planting cereal crops. The farmer can also plant potatoes or sugar beet.

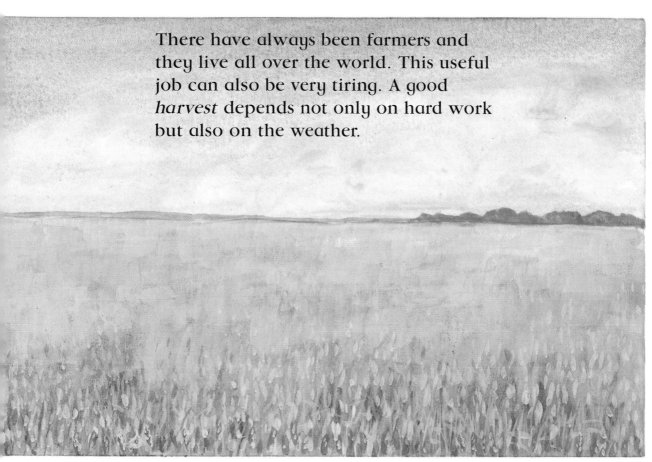

There have always been farmers and they live all over the world. This useful job can also be very tiring. A good *harvest* depends not only on hard work but also on the weather.

In summer and at *harvest*-time, farm labourers work from early morning until late at night when the weather is fine.

Farmers raise cattle, pigs, hens and other animals. They also grow many different crops.

The Craftsman

Craftsmen use the skill of their hands to make things. Some people work with leather, others with wood or metal. The result is like a painting or drawing – each object is unique, even though they may all look similar.

The joiner works with wood on a special workbench and makes furniture and other things using special tools.

The instrument-maker makes violins, guitars and cellos. Much skill and knowledge is needed to build an instrument that has a perfect sound.

The glass-blower uses a long blowpipe to shape *molten* glass into many different things, such as a vase or a glass.

The jeweller uses gold, silver and precious stones to create beautiful jewellery.

The Fisherman

When fishing conditions seem right, the fishermen throw a huge net, the trawl, into the sea. After several hours, they haul the net back on board and tip out the fish. When enough fish have been caught, the boat returns to port.

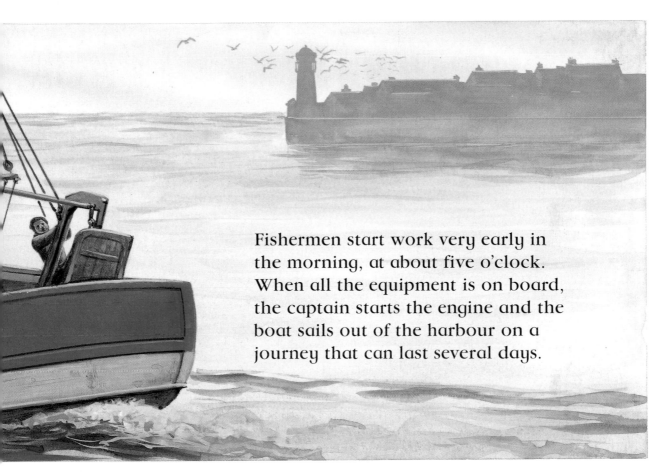

Fishermen start work very early in the morning, at about five o'clock. When all the equipment is on board, the captain starts the engine and the boat sails out of the harbour on a journey that can last several days.

Back in dock, the fishermen unload the fish and clean the boat and nets.

Fish are sold early each morning. Fishmongers from neighbouring towns come to buy fish from the fishermen.

Glossary

Airport
A place where aeroplanes take off and land. It is also where they are stored and maintained.

Barre
A level bar used in dance exercises.

Harvest
The collection of natural products that the farmer gathers, such as wheat, barley and fruit, is called the harvest.

Molten
Melted; made liquid.

Muscles
Muscles are found under our skin. They enable us to walk, run and jump.

Tranquillised
To be made calm.

X-ray
A special photograph of the inside of something, for example your body.